HARCOURT SCIENCE

WORKBOOK

TEACHER'S EDITION

Harcourt School Publishers

Orlando • Boston • Dallas • Chicago • San Diego

www.harcourtschool.com

Printed in the United States of America

ISBN 0-15-323718-X

3 4 5 6 7 8 9 10 022 10 09 08 07 06 05 04 03 02

Contents

UNIT A

Living Things Grow and Change

Chapter 1—Plants Grow and Change   WB1–WB10

Chapter 2—Animals Grow and Change   WB11–WB18

Chapter 3—People Grow and Change   WB19–WB30

UNIT B

Homes for Living Things

Chapter 1—Habitats for Plants and Animals   WB31–WB44

Chapter 2—Changes in Habitats   WB45–WB54

UNIT C

Exploring Earth's Surface

Chapter 1—Earth's Resources   WB55–WB64

Chapter 2—Earth Long Ago   WB65–WB74

UNIT D — Space and Weather

Chapter 1—The Solar System WB75–WB86

Chapter 2—Earth's Weather WB87–WB98

UNIT E — Exploring Matter

Chapter 1—Observing and Measuring Matter WB99–WB110

Chapter 2—Changes in Matter WB111–WB120

UNIT F — Energy in Motion

Chapter 1—Forces and Motion WB121–WB130

Chapter 2—Hearing Sound WB131–WB142

Introduction to Unit Experiments WB143–WB146

Unit A Experiment WB147–WB149

Unit B Experiment WB150–WB152

Unit C Experiment WB153–WB155

Unit D Experiment WB156–WB158

Unit E Experiment WB159–WB161

Unit F Experiment WB162–WB164

Science Safety

Think ahead.

Be neat.

Be careful.

Do not eat or drink things.

Safety Symbols

Be careful!

Sharp!

Be careful!

Wear an apron.

Wear goggles.

Science Safety

____ I will think ahead.

____ I will read the directions and follow them.

____ I will be neat with my materials.

____ I will take care of all science supplies.

____ I will clean up when I am done.

____ I will return all unused materials to my teacher.

____ I will be careful. I will follow all of the cautions.

____ I will not taste things I am using in an investigation unless my teacher tells me to

Name _____

Unit A, Chapter 1 Plants Grow and Change

LESSON 1 What Are Living and Nonliving Things?	LESSON 2 How Do Plants Grow and Change?	LESSON 3 How Are Plants Alike and Different?
Needs of Living Things	**How Plants Grow**	Pine Tree
1. food	1. Plants grow into _seedlings_	1. leaves like _needles_
2. _water_	2. Plants make leaves, _stems_, and _flowers_	2. seeds in _cones_
3. _air_	3. A fruit holds _seeds_	Oak Tree
What Living Things Do	**What Can Change Plants**	1. broad, flat _leaves_
1. grow	1. rain	2. seeds in _acorns_
2. _change_	2. sun	Cactus
	3. _insects_	1. stems store _water_
		2. leaves are _spines_

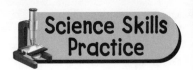

Compare

Write **living** or **nonliving** under each picture.

1. _____ nonliving

2. _____ living

3. _____ living

4. _____ nonliving

5. Use these words to complete the chart.

grow	do not grow	need water	do not need water

Living Things		Nonliving Things	
grow	need water	do not grow	do not need water

Use with page A4.

Name _____

What Are Living and Nonliving Things?

Complete the sentences. Use the words in the box.

living things	nonliving things	grow and change

1. Plants are _____*living things*_____ that need food, water, and air.

2. A puppy will _____*grow and change*_____ to become a dog.

3. Air and water are both _____*nonliving things*_____.

4. Mark an **X** on three things this rabbit needs to grow and change.

5. Mark an **X** on the things that will **not** grow.

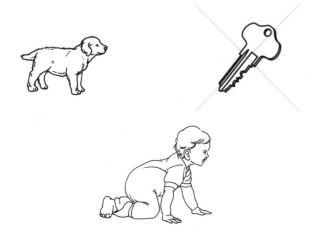

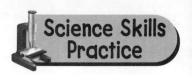
Science Skills
Practice

Observe

Plant 1   Plant 2

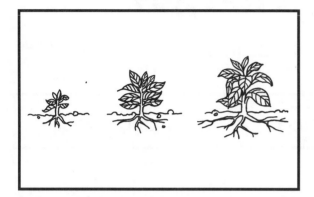 

1. Tell how Plant 1 grew. Color how you think it might look.

Plant 1 sprouted and grew. It looks healthy. It has lots
of leaves and a strong stem. Children should color all
the plants a healthy green.

2. Describe Plant 2. Color how you think it might look.

Plant 2 sprouted and grew. It didn't grow well. Its
stem is weak. Its leaves don't look healthy. Children
will probably color the young plant green and the
older plants yellow or brown.

3. Tell why you think Plant 2 looks the way it does.

Answers should indicate that Plant 2 did not get what it
needs to grow well. Based on their experiences in the
activity, most children will probably suggest that Plant
2 did not get enough water.

Name _____

How Do Plants Grow and Change?

Draw a line to match the words to each part of the plant.

1. Leaves make food. •

2. Stems hold up the plant and move water and nutrients through it. •

3. Roots take in water and nutrients from the soil. •

4. Flowers make seeds. •

Circle the term that best completes each sentence.

5. Most seeds are protected by a _____ .

seedling   (seed coat)

6. When a seed gets water and warmth, it may _____ .

die   (germinate)

7. As a plant grows, it _____ .

(changes)   germinates

8. This plant may die. Circle what is keeping the plant from making the food it needs.

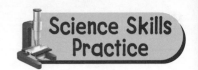

Classify

Classify the leaves into three groups. Draw the leaves you group together in the chart.

pine

black walnut

white birch

alder

honey locust

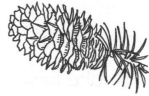
spruce

My Chart		
Needles	**One Large Leaf**	**Many Small Leaflets**
pine	white birch	honey locust
spruce	alder	black walnut

Use with page A14.

Concept
Review

How Are Plants
Alike and Different?

Draw a line to match the leaf to the plant
it came from.

1.

2.

3.

4. These plants grow in different parts of the world. Tell how
the plants are alike.

They have the same parts—roots, stems, and leaves.

_____

Both make their own food.

_____

Name _____

Plants Grow and Change

1. Label the parts of this seed. Use the words in the box.

tiny plant	stored food	seed coat

tiny plant _____   stored food _____

                                      seed coat _____

2. Draw an arrow to show where nutrients move through a plant.

Complete the sentences. Use the words in the box.

nutrients	germinate	plants

3. When a seed gets water and warmth, it may

_____germinate_____, or start to grow.

4. Minerals from the soil are _____nutrients_____.

5. All _____plants_____ grow and change.

Name _____

Cause and Effect

Read the paragraph. Then finish the chart below.

Mr. Smith's Garden

Mr. Smith had many seeds. He planted them in soil in his garden. He watered the seeds every day. Soon young plants began to grow. There were many sunny days, and Mr. Smith watered the plants every day. Soon they were fully grown. Then Mr. Smith had to go away for a few days. He hoped it would rain. It was very hot and sunny and the plants did not get water. When Mr. Smith returned, many of his plants had started to wilt. Mr. Smith gave the plants water and helped them become healthy again.

Cause	Effect
Mr. Smith watered the seeds every day.	Soon young plants began to grow.
It was very hot and sunny, and the plants did not get water.	The plants started to wilt.

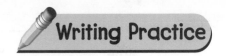

Describe a Plant

Write to Inform–Describe Look at a plant. Then write sentences that describe the parts of the plant. Tell what each part looks like and what it does. Use the outline to plan your sentences.

Plant part	What it looks like	What it does
_____ _____ _____	_____ _____ _____	_____ _____ _____
_____ _____ _____	_____ _____ _____	_____ _____ _____
_____ _____ _____	_____ _____ _____	_____ _____ _____
_____ _____ _____	_____ _____ _____	_____ _____ _____

Name _____

LESSON 1	LESSON 2
How Are Animals Different?	What Are Some Animal Life Cycles?
Five Kinds of Animals With Bones	Birds
1. mammals	1. hatch from eggs
2. birds	2. grow to look like their parents
3. amphibians	Mammals
4. reptiles	1. are born live
5. fish	2. grow to look like their parents
Four Kinds of Animals Without Bones	
1. insects	
2. spiders	
3. worms	
4. snails	

Unit A, Chapter 2 Animals Grow and Change

Name _____

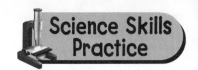

Classify

Classify these animals by how they are alike. Write your answers in the chart.

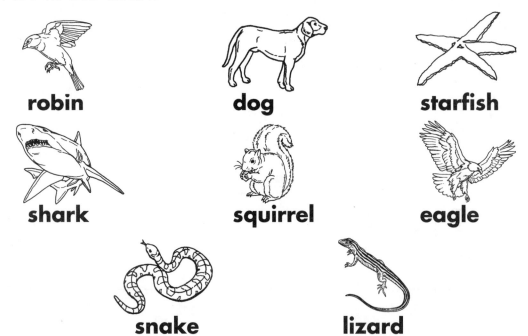

robin **dog** **starfish**

shark **squirrel** **eagle**

snake **lizard**

Have Fur	Can Fly	Live in Water	Have Scales
1. squirrel	2. robin	3. starfish	4. lizard
5. dog	6. eagle	7. shark	8. snake

Add another animal that belongs in each group. Write or draw your answers. Children's answers will vary.

9.	10.	11.	12.

How Are Animals
Alike and Different?

Match the word to the picture.

1. fish •

2. bird •

3. worm •

4. insect •

5. amphibian •

6. reptile •

7. mammal •

8. Circle the two animals above that do **not** have bones.

Name _____

Observe

What body parts are these animals using to help them survive? Write a sentence about how each animal uses a body part to live.

1. Possible answer: A goose uses wings to fly.

2. Possible answer: A frog uses legs to swim.

3. Possible answer: A fish uses gills to breathe or fins to swim.

What Are Some Animal Life Cycles?

1. The duck has laid her eggs. Tell what will happen to the eggs.

The ducklings in the shells are

alive. They grow and then hatch.

2. Draw what the duckling will look like when it is grown.

Drawing should look like an adult duck.

3. How is this bird caring for her young?

She is feeding them a worm.

4. What do animals do once they are grown?

Grown animals take care of themselves; they get their

own food and have their own young.

Name _____

Animals Grow and Change

Match the word to the words that tell about it.

1. mammal •   • Has rough, dry skin and scales

2. amphibian •   • Many have wings.

3. insect •   • Feeds milk to its young

4. reptile •   • Its body helps it live on land and water.

5. The pictures show the life cycle of a chicken. One picture is missing. Draw the missing picture. Then write sentences about what the pictures show.

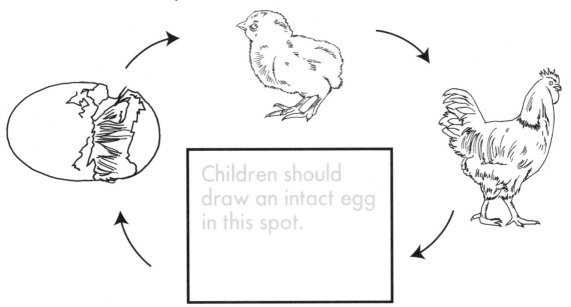

Children should draw an intact egg in this spot.

A chicken lays an egg. The egg hatches. The chick grows up and then lays eggs of its own.

_____

Name _____

Context Clues

Answer the questions.

What Kind of Animal Am I?

1. I have feathers to protect my body. I also have wings and a beak. What am I?

_____ bird _____

2. I have fur. I also make milk to feed my young. What am I?

_____ mammal _____

3. I live in water. I use gills to breathe and fins to swim. What am I?

_____ fish _____

Look at the animal. Use words to describe the animal.

Children's answers will vary.

_____

_____

_____

_____

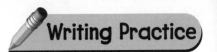
Writing Practice

Write a Song About Animals with Bones

Write to Express–Song Lyrics Write a song about four kinds of animals with bones. Your song should help people tell these animals apart. Include examples and descriptive words. Use the word web below to help you plan your song.

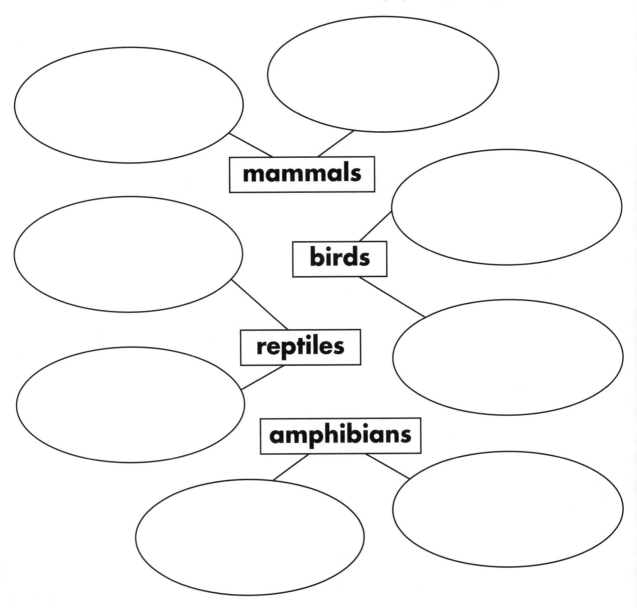

mammals

birds

reptiles

amphibians

Name _____

Unit A, Chapter 3 People Grow and Change

LESSON 1
How Will I Grow?

1. People grow and _change_

2. Permanent teeth _grow_

3. People learn _new things_

LESSON 2
What Do My Bones and Muscles Do?

1. Bones and muscles help you _move_

2. Some bones protect your _body_

3. The heart _is a muscle_

LESSON 3
How Do My Heart and Lungs Work?

1. The heart pumps blood to the _body_

2. The lungs help you _breathe_

3. The heart and lungs give the body _oxygen_

LESSON 4
How Do I Digest Food?

1. Food mixes with _saliva_ in the mouth.

2. Food moves to the _stomach_ and then to the _small intestine_

3. The Food Guide Pyramid helps you _choose healthful foods_

Name _____

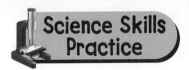

Predict

1. This is the mark left by Sandra's foot. How do you think her foot will look as she grows? Draw your answer.

foot should look progressively bigger

| Sandra's foot 1 year old | Sandra's foot 5 years old | Sandra's foot 20 years old |

2. Draw a picture of yourself now. Draw what you may look like when you grow up.

How I Look Now	How I May Look When I Grow Up

Use with page A42.

How Will I Grow?

Write on the lines how Juan will grow and change. Use the words in the box.

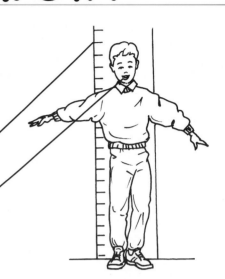

get taller   grow permanent teeth

1. get taller
_____

2. grow permanent teeth
_____

Label each person in the picture. Use the words in the box.

baby   child   teenager   adult

3. adult
_____

4. baby
_____

5. adult
_____

6. teenager
_____

7. child
_____

8. How is Chris learning?
Chris is reading.
_____

Name _____

Science Skills Practice

Make a Model

1. Draw what Robby will look like when all of his permanent teeth grow in.
Picture should show a mouthful of permanent teeth.

2. Mark an **X** on the mouth that belongs to a small child.

What Do My Bones and Muscles Do?

Write **move** or **protect** to tell about each
bone or group of bones.

1. skull— protect
   _____

2. ribs— protect
   _____

3. arm bones— move
   _____

4. hand bones— move
   _____

5. leg bones— move
   _____

6. foot bones— move
   _____

Your Bones

7. Tell what the muscle pair does to
   help this arm move.

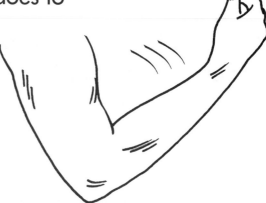

One muscle pulls the bone one way to move the arm up.
_____
The other muscle pulls the bone the other way to move
_____
the arm down.
_____

Observe

1. Color the skeleton **blue**.
Color the muscles **red**.
All bones should be blue.
Muscles should be red.

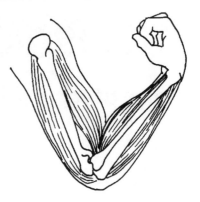

2. These children are playing kickball. Circle the
muscles that help them move.

arm muscles

leg muscles

foot muscles

3. Tell how this boy is keeping his
bones and muscles healthy.
He is eating a healthful snack.

_____

_____

_____

Use with page A54.

How Do My Heart and Lungs Work?

Complete the sentences. Use the words in the box.

| blood | oxygen |

1. Your heart pumps _____blood_____ to all parts of your body.

2. When you breathe in, your lungs take in _____oxygen_____.

3. Draw arrows to show where the heart pumps blood.

Arrows should be from heart to all parts of body.

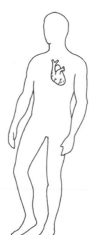

4. Circle the girl who probably has a faster heart rate. Tell how she is helping her heart and lungs stay healthy.

She is exercising.

_____

Name _____

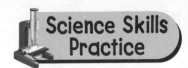

Observe

1. Write three body parts that
help this boy chew his food.

face muscles
_____

teeth
_____

face bones
_____

2. Circle the food that has to be chewed. Tell why.

The apple has to be chewed so it is broken down

before it is swallowed.
_____

_____

_____

How Do I Digest Food?

Label the picture. Use the words in the box.

esophagus	mouth	saliva
large intestine	stomach	small intestine

1. mouth (or saliva)

2. saliva (or mouth)

3. esophagus

4. stomach

5. small intestine

6. large intestine

7. Show how food moves through the body. Draw an arrow on the picture above. Arrow should be from mouth, through esophagus, into stomach and intestines.

8. What does saliva do to food?
Saliva starts to digest food.

9. What happens to food in the stomach?
In the stomach, food mixes with special juices and turns into a liquid.

Name _____

People Grow and Change

Match the body part to the word that describes it.

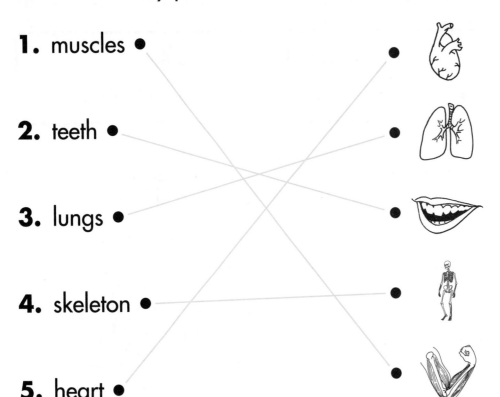

1. muscles •

2. teeth •

3. lungs •

4. skeleton •

5. heart •

Circle **true** or **false**. If the answer is false, change the underlined word to make it true.

6. Your <u>heart rate</u> is how fast or slow your heart beats.

(true) false _____

7. Saliva in your <u>stomach</u> begins to break down food.

true (false) mouth _____

8. To get energy and nutrients, your body must digest <u>air</u>.

true (false) food _____

Name _____

Relate Pictures to Text

Food Guide Pyramid The Food Guide Pyramid can help you choose healthful foods to eat. There are six food groups. Grains such as bread and cereal are at the bottom of the pyramid. Foods you should eat the most of are from this group. Other groups include fruits, vegetables, milk, meat, and fats. Foods you should eat the least of are from the fats group.

Use the paragraph and picture to help you answer the questions.

1. What kinds of foods are in the vegetable group?

Sample answers: peas, carrots, potatoes, and corn
_____

2. Ice cream and cottage cheese are in what group?

the milk, yogurt, and cheese group
_____

3. What might be some healthful breakfast foods?

Sample answer: a bowl of cereal with milk, a banana,
_____
and a piece of toasted wheat bread
_____

Use with page A62. | **Workbook • WB29**

Explain a Lost Tooth

Write to Inform–Explanation Pretend that a first grader is surprised by losing a baby tooth. Write an explanation. Tell why baby teeth fall out and what will happen next. Answer the questions below to help you plan your writing.

Why do humans lose baby teeth?

Accept children's answers. _____

_____

When do people usually begin to lose baby teeth?

_____

_____

What happens to cause baby teeth to fall out?

_____

_____

What will happen after a baby tooth falls out?

_____

_____

How can you take care of new teeth?

_____

_____

Name _____

Unit B, Chapter 1 Habitats for Plants and Animals

LESSON 1
What Is a Habitat?

1. An animal's habitat is the place where it __lives__.

2. Animals meet their needs in __habitats__.

LESSON 2
What Are Different Land Habitats?

Land Habitats

1. __desert habitats__

2. __rain forest habitats__

3. __forest habitats__

4. __tundra habitats__

LESSON 3
What Are Different Water Habitats?

Water Habitats

1. __freshwater pond__

2. __saltwater ocean__

LESSON 4
What Are Some Animal Adaptations?

1. changing __color__

2. moving and __migrating__

3. responding to heat and __cold__

LESSON 5
How Do Plants and Animals Help Each Other?

1. Animals use plants for food and __shelter__.

2. Animals help move __seeds__.

Name _____

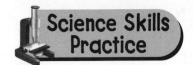

Communicate

Children may color things used for food, water, or shelter.

1. Color two things this squirrel needs to live.   The squirrel
also needs air.

2. Tell how the squirrel meets its needs.

Answers will vary. Children may indicate that the

squirrel gathers nuts for food, gets water from

the river, or finds shelter in the forest. Accept

reasonable answers.

_____

_____

_____

Name _____

What Is a Habitat?

Match each animal to its habitat.

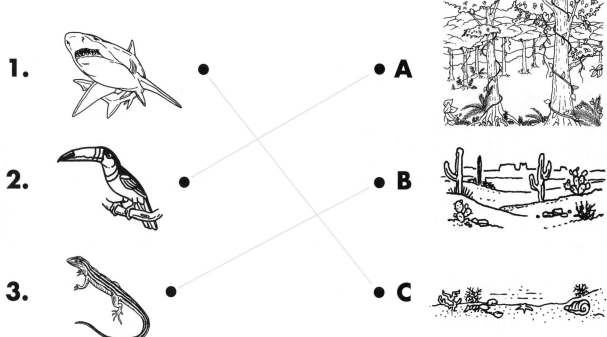

1. • • A

2. • • B

3. • • C

This is the bear's habitat. Write two things from this habitat that the bear needs to live.

4. food or fish _____   5. water or stream _____

Some children may also suggest shelter or air.

Name _____

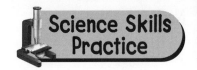

Classify

Write **land** or **water** to tell the environment
in which the animal lives.

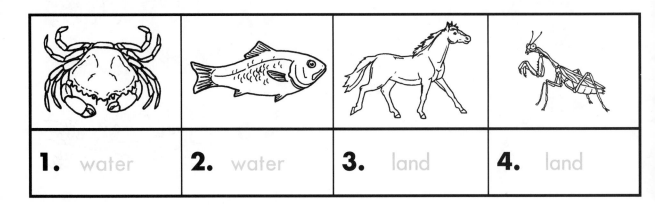

1. water	**2.** water	**3.** land	**4.** land

Match each animal to its habitat. The habitats will be used
more than one time.

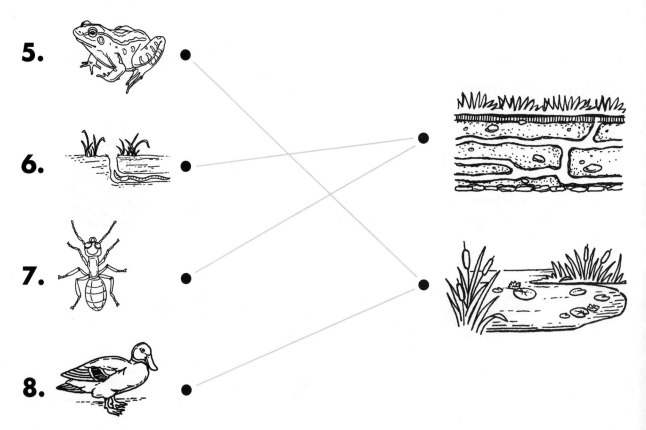

5.

6.

7.

8.

Name _____

What Are Different Land Habitats?

Circle the word or words that tell about each habitat.

1. desert   (dry)   wet

2. rain forest   dry   (wet)

3. forest   (many plants)   few plants

4. tundra   many plants   (few plants)

Circle the plants and animals that grow in hot, wet habitats.

5.

6.

7.

8.

9.

10.

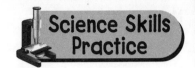

Predict

This is a northern city park in summer. What will the park look like in winter? Draw your prediction.

Drawings should show trees with no leaves; empty nest; no flowers or butterflies; pond may be frozen over; there may be snow. Accept reasonable predictions.

Use with page B14.

Name _____

What Are Different Water Habitats?

Pretend that you are a scientist who studies ponds.
In each box, draw or write about one living thing
you might observe in this pond.

1.

2.

3.

4.

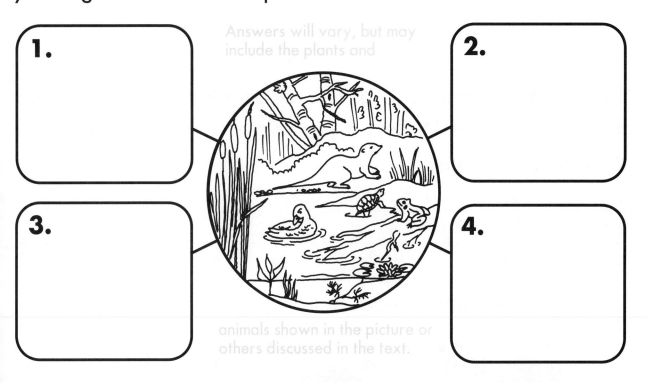

Answers will vary, but may include the plants and

animals shown in the picture or others discussed in the text.

5. Circle the animals that come to the surface to breathe.

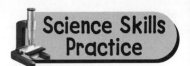

Form a Hypothesis

This is nature in winter. A brown rabbit and a white rabbit are sitting in the snow. Write a hypothesis about which rabbit can be seen more easily.

I can see the brown rabbit better than the white rabbit in the snow.

This is nature in fall. A brown rabbit and a white rabbit are sitting in the leaves on the ground. Write a hypothesis about which rabbit can be seen more easily.

I can see the white rabbit better than the brown rabbit in the leaves.

Name _____

What Are Some Animal Adaptations?

Animals have different ways of adapting to their environments. On the line, write the way each animal adapts to its environment.

1. hibernating _____

2. migrating _____

3. estivating _____

4. camouflage _____

5. body covering _____

6. In what season do animals estivate? summer _____

7. Why do animals move? Animals move to find food or _____ to get away from danger. _____

Name _____

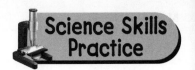

Observe

Look at the habitats. Complete the chart to tell what
you observe.

Tundra

Rain Forest

	Tundra	**Rain Forest**
Plants	few, small ones	trees bushes vines
Animals	polar bear seal	monkey bird

Use with page B28.

Name _____

Concept Review

How Do Plants and Animals Help Each Other?

1. Mark an **X** on the animals using plants as food. Circle the animals using plants as shelter.

2. Color the animal helping a plant grow in a new place. Tell how you know.

The deer has seeds stuck to its fur. The seeds may be
_____
dropped as the deer moves from place to place.
_____

3. Color all the parts of the ocean food chain. Circle the parts that start the food chain. Children should color the plants, small fish, larger fish, and shark; they should circle the plants.

Habitats for Plants and Animals

Solve the riddles. Use the words in the box.

tundra	desert	rain forest	forest

1. Joseph is in a place that is hot and dry.
Where is he? desert _____

2. Brittany is in a place that is hot and wet.
Where is she? rain forest _____

3. Michael is in a place that is cold and windy.
Where is he? tundra _____

4. Ana is in a place where the trees lose their leaves in winter.
Where is she? forest _____

Circle **true** or **false**. If the sentence is false, change the underlined term to make the sentence true.

5. An <u>adaptation</u> is anything that helps an animal live in its environment.
(true) false _____

6. A <u>pond</u> is a small body of fresh water.
(true) false _____

7. A <u>camouflage</u> is where a living thing can get what it needs to live.   true (false) habitat _____

          Use with pages B4–B33.

Name _____

Distinguish Between Fact and Nonfact

Facts About Water Habitats

Earth has many water environments. Most ponds are freshwater environments. Snapping turtles, muskrats, and many kinds of insects live along the banks of a pond. Plants that grow on the surface of a pond are used by these animals for food. Ducks float on the surface of a pond. They eat insects that float on the water.

Look at the chart. Mark an **X** in the box to tell whether the sentence is a **fact** or a **nonfact** from the above paragraph.

	Fact	Nonfact
All ponds are saltwater environments.		X
Earth has few water environments.		X
Animals use plants that grow on the surface of a pond for food.	X	
Muskrats live along the banks of a pond.	X	
Ducks eat insects that float on the water.	X	

Name _____

Describe a Food Chain

Write to Inform—Description Think of a food chain in a forest or a lake. Draw a diagram showing three steps of the food chain. Write one sentence to describe each step of the food chain. Use the outline below to help you plan your writing.

Diagram	Sentences
	Accept reasonable answers.

Name _____

Unit B, Chapter 2 Changes in Habitats

LESSON 1 How Does Weather Change Habitats?	LESSON 2 How Does Pollution Change Environments?	LESSON 3 How Do People Help the Environment?
1. Too little rain— droughts	Kinds of Pollution	Parts of Environment
2. Too much rain— floods	1. land	1. land
3. Lightning— forest fires	2. air	2. air
	3. water	3. water

Name _____

Draw a Conclusion

Plant A   **Plant B**

1. Describe each plant.

Plant A	Plant B
healthy	wilted, dying

2. Why do you think Plant B looks the way it does?

It is not getting the water it needs to live.

_____

_____

3. What might help Plant B?

water

_____

Name _____

How Does Weather Change Habitats?

1. Color the things that could die from drought **yellow**.
Color the things that move to other ponds because of
drought **blue**. Plants and fish should be yellow; frog and
snake should be blue.

2. This forest has burned. Tell how the birds might help
the forest.
They drop seeds to start new plants.

_____

_____

Name _____

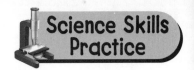

Observe

X should be on all litter.

1. Some things in this park don't belong. Mark an **X** on all the things people can clean up.

2. What are some things you can do to help keep the outdoors clean?

Answers will vary but may include throwing trash in
_____
trash cans.
_____

_____

_____

Concept Review

How Does Pollution Change Environments?

These things were found on the ground in a forest.
Mark an **X** on things that are pollution.

1. leaf

2. juice carton

3. pine cone

4. tire

5. milk jug

6. flower

7. How might these fish be harmed by pollution?

They can get caught in the plastic
and have trouble moving. They
can be hurt by factory waste.

8. Think about how you can keep a habitat clean. Draw a
picture to go with your idea.

Name _____

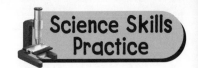

Communicate

1. You have yarn, markers, empty boxes, buttons, and a plastic jug. Draw something new you could make using these materials.

2. Write steps to tell how you would make your object.

Step 1: _Children should describe a step-by-step_
_____
process for making an object. Look for

Step 2: _logical reasoning and clear directions._
_____

_____

Step 3: _____

_____

Concept Review

How Do People Help the Environment?

Label each object with the bin it belongs in. Use the letters **A**, **B**, **C**, and **D**.

PAPER A	GLASS B	METAL C	PLASTIC D

1. ____ C (metal)   2. ____ A (paper)   3. ____ B (glass)

4. ____ D (plastic)   5. ____ D (plastic)   6. ____ A (paper)

Circle the better choice for each question.

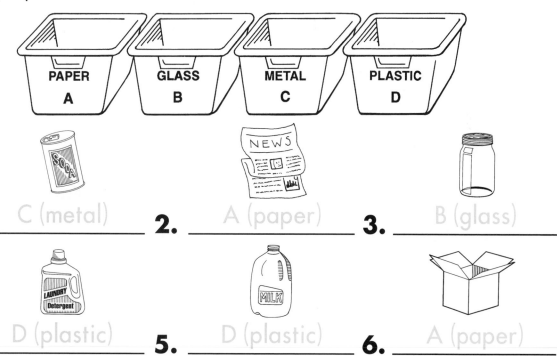

7. How can someone help keep the air clean?

8. How can someone help keep the water clean?

9. How can someone help keep the playground clean?

Changes in Habitats

Circle the word that completes each sentence about Jack.

1. Jack will _____ the cup.   (reuse)   return

2. Jack is helping solve _____ problems.

party   (pollution)

Write the word that best completes each sentence.

drought	litter	recycle	reuse

3. You can _____reuse_____ an empty milk jug to hold water for plants.

4. You can _____recycle_____ newspaper to make new paper.

5. Trash in water or on the ground is _____litter_____.

6. Too little rain can cause a _____drought_____.

Name _____

Predict Outcomes

The Picnic Jane and her family are having a picnic lunch.
They are eating sandwiches, chips, and soft drinks. Sometimes
Jane's brothers can leave a big mess. Jane tells them not to
litter. Jane knows that litter can harm plants and animals.
Suddenly it begins to rain. Jane and her family quickly pack
up the picnic and go home.

1. What kind of mess could Jane's family leave?

They could leave litter in the form of empty packages

and containers.

2. What might happen if Jane's brothers don't listen to Jane
and they leave litter behind?

Plants and animals could be harmed by the litter.

3. When the family leaves so quickly, they forget to throw
away the plastic holder from the drink cans. What might
happen to the animals that live in that environment?

The animals could get trapped inside the plastic

holder from the drink cans.

Tell a Recycling Story

Write to Express–Narrative Pretend that you are something that will be reused in a recycling project. Write a story that tells what you were first used for, how you were recycled, and what you are used for now. Use the story map below to help you plan your story.

What are you?   _____   _____
What were you used for first?   _____   _____
How were you recycled?   _____   _____
What are you used for now?   _____   _____

Name _____

Unit C, Chapter 1 Earth's Resources

LESSON 1 How Do People Use Rocks and Soil?	LESSON 2 How Do People Use Plants?	LESSON 3 How Do People Use Water?
Some Uses of Rocks **1.** build houses and _roads_ **2.** make _sculptures_ **Some Uses of Soil** **1.** grow _food_ **2.** make _bricks_	**Some Uses of Plants** **1.** houses and _furniture_ **2.** _paper_ **3.** _clothing_ **4.** _fuel_ **5.** food and _medicine_	**Some Uses of Water** **1.** drinking and _cooking_ **2.** bathing and _washing_ **3.** _transportation_ **4.** _electricity_

Name _____

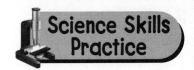

Infer

1. These clothes have just been washed, and they are wet. Infer why the clothes have been hung on a line.

The air and sun will help them dry.

_____

_____

2. Soil was used to build this brick house. Infer how the soil was changed to make bricks.

The soil was shaped and dried to form bricks.

_____

_____

How Do People Use Rocks and Soil?

1. Color all the things that could be made from rocks.

Children should color everything but the fence.

wall   **fence**   **statue**   **beach**

Complete each sentence with words from the box.

soil	rock	resource	natural resource

2. A ____natural____ ____resource____ is something found in nature that people can use to meet their needs.

3. A ____rock____ is a hard, nonliving thing that comes from the Earth.

4. A ____resource____ is anything that people can use.

5. The loose top layer of the Earth's surface is ____soil____.

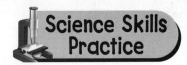
Science Skills Practice

Communicate

Pretend you are telling younger children how to clean their hands. Write what you would say.

Step 1. Wet your hands.

Step 2. Use soap.

Step 3. Rinse your hands.

Step 4. Dry your hands.

5. Pretend you are going away on vacation for one week. Your friend is going to take care of your plant. Finish the note to your friend.

Please _water_ _____ my plant!

How Do People Use Plants?

1. Circle all the things that come from or are made from plants.

2. Color the things that are plants.

Children should color the aloe plant and the tree.

3. Tell how plants are being used in each picture.

to build a campfire   to make cloth   to provide food

4. Write a few sentences describing your favorite foods that come from plants.

Children's answers will vary, but they should list foods

that come from plants. They should list fruits and

vegetables mainly.

_____

_____

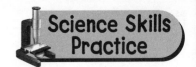
Science Skills Practice

Collect Data

Tell how this family is using water. Record your answers in the chart.

MOM   DAVE MIKE   DAD   SUSAN

Person	How Person Is Using Water	
Susan	1.	to get cool (or recreation)
Mom	2.	to wash the car
Dad	3.	to water the garden
Mike	4.	to drink
Dave	5.	to drink

List four more ways people use water. Accept reasonable answers.

6. _____   7. _____

8. _____   9. _____

Name _____

Concept Review

How Do People Use Water?

Mark an **X** on the things that are using water to live.

1.

2.

3.

4.

5.

6.

Tell how these people are using water.

7. for fishing (or fun)
_____
_____

8. for transportation
_____
(or fun)

Use with page C17.

Workbook • WB61

Earth's Resources

Complete each sentence with words from the box.

rock	soil	resource	natural resource
	medicine	transportation	

1. A nonliving thing that comes from the Earth is a ___rock___.

2. A _natural resource_ is something found in nature that people use to meet their needs.

3. Cars, boats, and bicycles are kinds of _transportation_.

4. A _medicine_ is a product that helps people who are ill.

5. People use ___soil___ to grow food.

6. Anything that people can use is a _resource_.

Tell the purpose of each picture. Use words from the box.

natural resource	transportation	medicine

7. _transportation_   **8.** _natural resource_   **9.** _medicine_

Name _____

Arrange Events in Sequence

The Process of Making Paper

Numbers show the order in which things happened. Show the order of events by putting a number beside each picture.

__2__

__1__

__4__

__3__

__6__

__5__

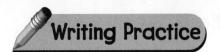

Write a Resource Poem

Write to Express–Poem Think of a resource. Write a poem that describes the resource. Use the word web below to help you plan your poem.

How it looks	Where it is found

Resource

Why you like it	How people use it

Name _____

Unit C, Chapter 2 Earth Long Ago

LESSON 1 What Is a Fossil?	LESSON 2 What Have Scientists Learned from Fossils?	LESSON 3 What Have Scientists Learned About Dinosaurs?
1. A _fossil_ is what is left of a plant or animal that lived long ago. 2. It takes millions of years to _make fossils_ . 3. Fossils are found in rock, _amber_ , and _tar_ .	What Scientists Use Fossils to Learn About 1. _plants_ of long ago 2. _animals_ of long ago	Kind of Dinosaurs 1. large and _small_ 2. meat eaters and _plant eaters_

Name _____

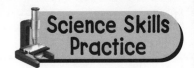

Science Skills
Practice

Infer

Match each print to the object that made it.

1. •   •

2. •   •

3. •   •

4. •   •

5. Three people made prints with their feet in the wet cement. Match each set of footprints to the person who made them.

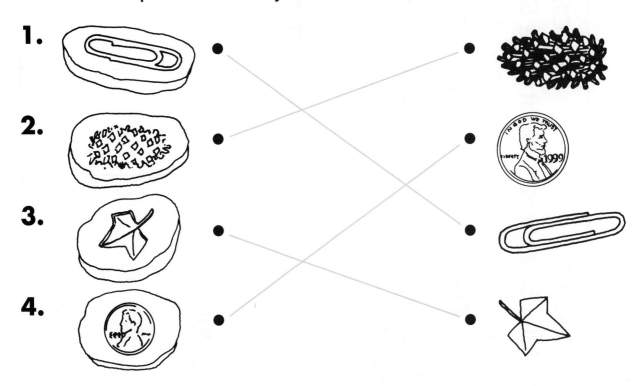

6. How did you make your choices?

Children will likely have matched the people with the

size of the feet and the shoe style of the print.

_____

WB66 • Workbook   **Use with page C24.**

What Is a Fossil?

Match each word to the fossil it would make.

1. shell •

2. leaf •

3. animal •

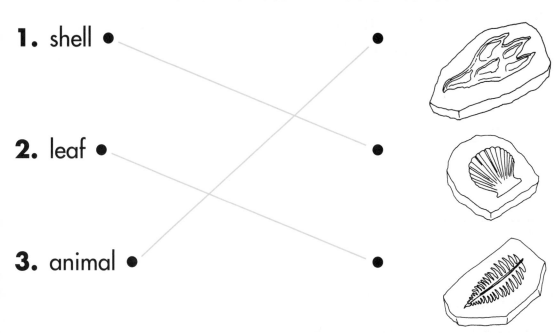

Fossils can be found in different places. List three fossils a paleontologist could find in these layers of rock.

4. fish _____

5. shells _____

6. leaves (or plants) _____

Name _____

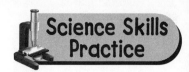
Communicate

1. Pretend you are a paleontologist. You have three rocks that have fossils in them. Tell someone what you would do to find and clean the fossils.

Answers will vary but should include steps taken in the

investigation, such as using tools to chip away rock

from fossils and using a brush to clean the fossils.

_____

_____

These three rocks have different kinds of fossils. Draw what each fossil would look like. Share your drawings with a classmate.

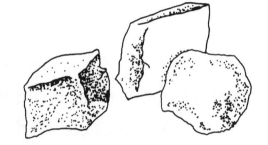

Check children's pictures.

2. plant fossil   **3.** footprint fossil   **4.** shell fossil

Name _____

What Have Scientists Learned from Fossils?

Match the dinosaur fossils with the pictures that show how the dinosaurs might have looked.

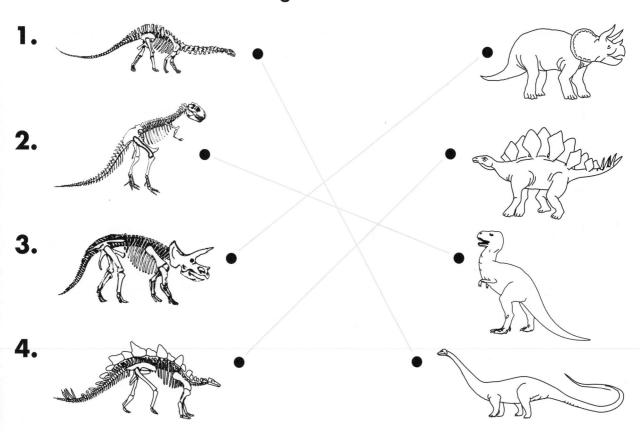

1.

2.

3.

4.

5. Describe what paleontologists do.

Answers may vary. Paleontologists find fossils; they put
them together; they study them; they compare them to
plants and animals today to see how plants and animals
have changed.

_____

Name _____

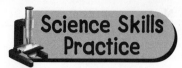

Make a Model

1. Examine the plastic bones.
In the box, draw a model
of the assembled skeleton.

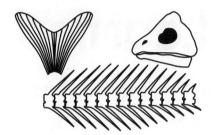

Children should show an assembled fish skeleton.

2. What kind of animal left the skeleton? _____fish_____

3. When paleontologists find dinosaur bones, they put them together. Color the picture that shows which dinosaur these bones belong to. Children should color the stegosaurus.

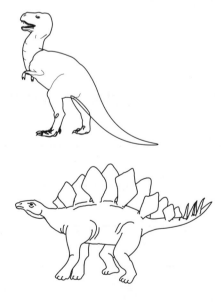

Name _____

What Have Scientists Learned About Dinosaurs?

1. Circle the dinosaur that was a large meat eater.

Triceratops   (Tyrannosaurus rex)

2. Draw the correct kind of teeth on the dinosaurs below.
Meat eaters should have sharp pointed teeth; plant eaters

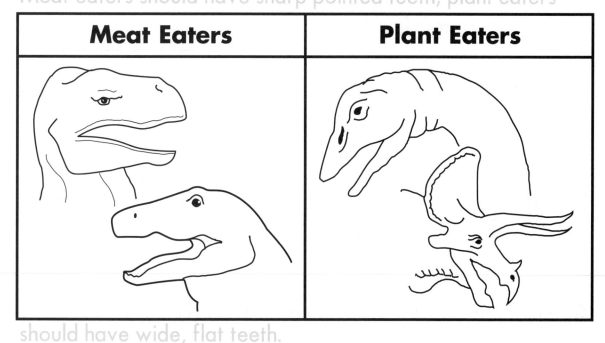

Meat Eaters	Plant Eaters

should have wide, flat teeth.

3. Mark an **X** on the animal that has skin that is most like a dinosaur's skin.

Name _____

Earth Long Ago

Circle **true** or **false**. If the sentence is false,
change the underlined word to make it true.

dinosaur	paleontologists	extinct	reconstruct

1. What is left of a plant or animal
from long ago is a <u>fossil</u>.

(true)   false

_____

2. Paleontologists sometimes <u>extinct</u>
bones to see what an animal
might have looked like.

true   (false)

reconstruct

3. When every one of a kind of
animal is no longer alive,
it is <u>a fossil</u>.

true   (false)

extinct

4. Fill in the blanks with the correct words.

When ____paleontologists____ find ____dinosaur____

bones, they rebuild them to study things about that animal.

5. Make a drawing
of a leaf fossil.

Check children's
drawings.

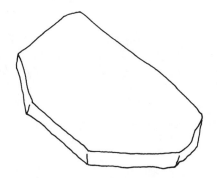

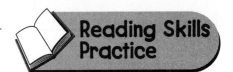

Use Prefixes to Determine Word Meaning

Fossils

Look at the underlined word in each sentence. Draw a line around the sentence that does not make sense.

1. Scientists <u>deconstruct</u>, or rebuild, as much of a fossil as possible. should be circled

Scientists <u>reconstruct</u>, or rebuild, as much of a fossil as possible.

2. Scientists often have to <u>remove</u> a fossil from rock.

Scientists often have to <u>move</u> a fossil from rock. should be circled

A word in each sentence is missing a prefix. Use a prefix from the box and add it to the word to make it correct.

pre	re

3. To __re__ build means to build again.

4. To __pre__ pare means to get ready.

Write a sentence using the word <u>rebuild</u>.

Accept sentences that correctly use the word *rebuild*.

_____

Compare and Contrast Dinosaurs

Write to Inform—Compare and Contrast Pretend that you work in a natural history museum. Some young children want to know how to tell a Stegosaurus from a Tyrannosaurus rex. Write a few sentences that compare and contrast these two dinosaurs. Use the Venn diagram below to help you plan your sentences.

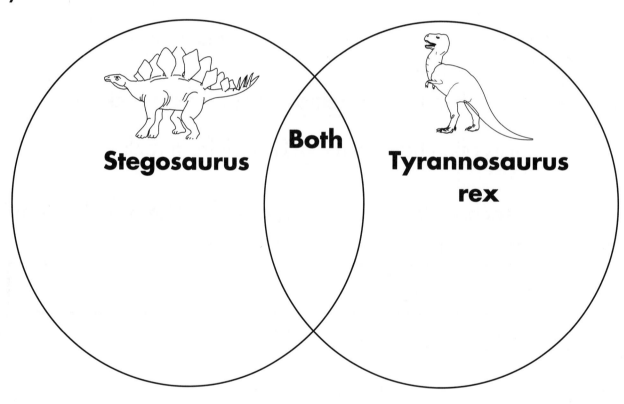

Stegosaurus   **Both**   **Tyrannosaurus rex**

Accept reasonable answers.

_____

_____

_____

Unit D, Chapter 1 The Solar System

LESSON 1
What Are Stars and Planets?

1. The solar system consists of the sun and nine planets.

2. A group of stars that form a picture is called a constellation .

LESSON 2
What Causes Day and Night?

1. Earth rotates about every 24 hours .

2. Earth's rotation causes each part of Earth to have light and dark each day.

LESSON 3
What Causes the Seasons?

1. Earth's tilt is always the same .

2. Earth orbits the sun .

LESSON 4
How Does the Moon Move and Change?

1. It takes the moon about four weeks to orbit Earth .

2. The moon's orbit makes it appear to change shape .

Name _____

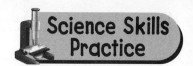

Communicate

Draw lines to connect the stars. Tell what
shape each picture is.

1. apple _____ **2.** arrow _____ **3.** heart _____

4. Write a sentence that tells about all three pictures.
Accept reasonable answers. Connecting the dots
showed a picture, just like connecting stars shows
pictures in the sky.

5. Make up your own shape. Draw lines to connect
some or all of the stars.

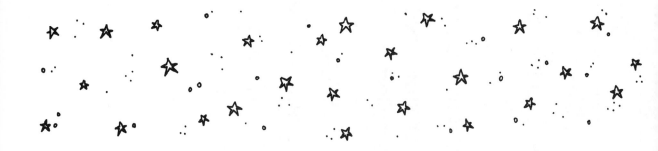

6. Tell about the picture you made.
Accept reasonable answers.
_____
_____

Name _____

What Are Stars and Planets?

Underline all the sentences that are **true**.

1. <u>Stars are much bigger than Earth.</u>

2. Planets give off their own light.

3. <u>Some stars look brighter because they are closer to Earth.</u>

4. Cross out anything you can **not** see in the night sky.

planets   ~~the sun~~   stars   the moon

What Is the Solar System?

Complete the sentences below by choosing a word from the box.

planet	nine	solar system	star

5. The sun is a _____ star _____.

6. A _____ planet _____ is a large ball of rock or gas that moves around the sun.

7. Together, the sun and the planets make up the _____ solar system _____.

8. There are _____ nine _____ planets in our solar system.

Name _____

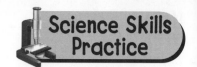
Time/Space Relationships

1. Mark an **X** on everything that looks far away from the house.

2. The two balls in the picture are the same size. Tell why one looks smaller.

One looks smaller because it is farther away.

_____

3. Draw a penny close up in Box A. Draw a penny far away in Box B.

Box A   Box B

The penny in Box B should be smaller.

What Causes Day and Night?

Draw a line under each sentence that is **true**.

1. The sun is a star.

2. The sun is made of hot gases.

3. The sun moves around Earth.

4. We get heat and light from the sun.

5. The girl in the boxes is rotating. Draw what she will look like next. Children should draw the girl facing away from them.

6. Circle the things that rotate.

top

merry-go-round

tree

Earth

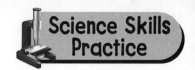
Observe

1. This picture shows the sun and Earth.
Color the part of Earth the sun is shining on.
Children should color the left half.

Complete the sentences.

2. On the lighted side of Earth, it is _____ day _____.

3. On the dark side of Earth, it is _____ night _____.

Name _____

What Causes the Seasons?

1. Draw a line to show the path Earth follows around the sun. Drawing should indicate an oval around the sun.

2. Earth's path around the sun is called an ___orbit___.

Circle the missing word.

3. Earth goes around the sun once each _____.

day   week   month   (year)

4. Pretend you live where the **X** is on this Earth. Label each season. Summer has been done for you.

spring
_____

summer
_____

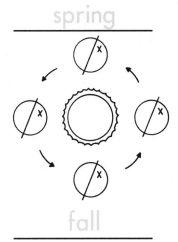

winter
_____

fall
_____

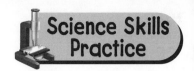

Compare

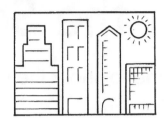

1. Compare the pictures of the city. Tell how the pictures are the same and different.

The Same	Different
Both show the same buildings.	At night the moon is in the sky, and people must use lights to see. In the day the sun is shining. The sun makes the city bright.

2. One picture shows summer. The other shows winter. Label each picture. Tell how you knew.

summer   winter

The summer picture shows people in warm weather.

The winter picture shows a person wearing winter

clothes. Accept reasonable answers.

Name _____

How Does the Moon Move and Change?

1. Circle the ending that will make a true sentence.

The moon _____.

    A gives off its own light   **B** reflects the sun's light

2. Sometimes rocks from space hit the moon. They make craters. Draw craters on the moon.

Children should draw circles on the moon to represent craters.

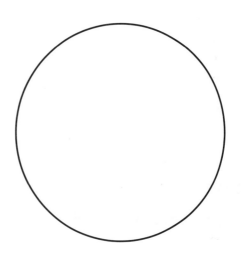

3. The pictures show how the moon changes during a month. Color in the moons to show the shapes that are missing.

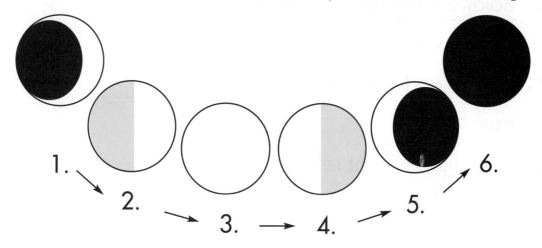

1.   2.   3.   4.   5.   6.

Vocabulary Review

The Solar System

Match each picture to the word that tells about it.

1. crater ●

2. constellation ●

3. rotation ●

4. orbit ●

Circle **true** or **false**. If a sentence is false,
change the **underlined** word to make it true.

5. The <u>moon</u> is the star closest to Earth.

   true   (false) sun _____

6. <u>Solar energy</u> is light and heat.

   (true)   false _____

7. Winter and summer are <u>seasons</u>.

   (true)   false _____

8. Moonlight is light reflected from the <u>sun</u>.

   (true)   false _____

Name _____

Cause and Effect

The Seasons

As Earth orbits the sun, seasons change. When a part of Earth faces the sun directly and gets more sunlight, it is summer there. The air feels warm, and there are many green plants. Sometimes it is rainy. When a part of Earth does not get light as directly, it is winter there. It is usually much colder in winter. The trees are bare, and sometimes it snows. Often lakes and ponds freeze and turn to ice.

What is the effect of each cause? Finish the chart below.

Cause	Effect
Earth orbits the sun.	The seasons change.
Part of Earth faces the sun directly.	It is summer.
It is summer.	The air feels warm, there are many green plants, and sometimes it rains.
Part of Earth does not get direct sunlight.	It is winter.

Describe a Planet

Write to Inform—Description Choose a planet other than Earth from our solar system. Write a paragraph that describes the planet for a children's reference book. Use the outline below to help you plan your paragraph.

Planet name	Place in the solar system
Size and color of the planet	Hot or cold
Other interesting facts about the planet	

Unit D, Chapter 2 Earth's Weather

LESSON 2

What Is the Water Cycle?

1. Water _evaporates_ into the air.

2. Water vapor changes into tiny _water drops_ that form _clouds_ .

3. The water drops fall as _rain_ or _snow_ .

LESSON 4

How Can We Prepare for Weather?

Kinds of Storms

1. _thunderstorm_
2. _tornado_
3. _hurricane_
4. _blizzard_

LESSON 1

How Does Weather Change?

1. Weather can change from _day to day_ .

2. Weather changes _with the seasons_ .

LESSON 3

How Do We Measure Weather Conditions?

1. Scientists use tools to measure _weather conditions_ .

2. Clouds help people predict _weather_ .

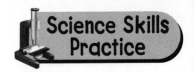

Observe

1. Draw the picture that matches each day's weather.
Use the pictures in the key.

KEY:

| sunny | partly sunny | cloudy | stormy |

Monday	**Tuesday**	**Wednesday**	**Thursday**
sunny	cloudy	partly sunny	stormy
Check children's drawings.			

2. Draw something you might do on a cold, sunny day.
Write about your picture.

Check children's drawings.

Accept reasonable answers.

_____

_____

Name _____

How Does Weather Change?

Each set of words tells about the kind of weather a season may have. Match the words to the season.

1. fall •   • warm and wet

2. winter •   • hot and sunny

3. spring •   • cool and some plants die

4. summer •   • cold with snow

Each picture shows something about the weather.
Draw how the weather can change.

5.    Possible drawing: drop in temperature and clouds over sun

6.    Possible drawing: flag waving in a stiff breeze

7.    Possible drawing: rain falling from clouds

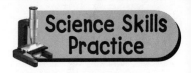

Infer

What do you think will happen? Draw what you think.

Answers should indicate condensation on the glass in the sunlight.

Jar at Beginning

Jar After 30 Minutes

1. This jar is in a sunny window. Draw how you think the jar will change.

sun

2. This jar is in a shady place. Draw how you think the jar will change.

The jar will not change.

shade

3. Draw what might happen next.

Children should draw rain falling.

Use with page D42.

What Is the Water Cycle?

Circle **true** or **false**. If the sentence is false, change the
underlined term to make it true.

1. Heat from the sun makes water
  <u>evaporate</u>.

(true)   false

_____

2. Clouds are made of <u>water vapor</u>.

true   (false)

tiny drops of water

_____

3. Label each part of the water cycle. Use the letters
  in the box. **A** has been labeled for you.

A Water evaporates.
B Water vapor cools and changes to tiny drops of water.
C Water drops come together to form clouds.
D Drops in clouds get too heavy and fall as rain.

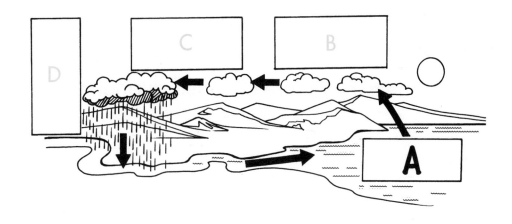

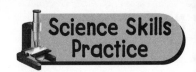

Use Data

This graph shows the temperature for five days.

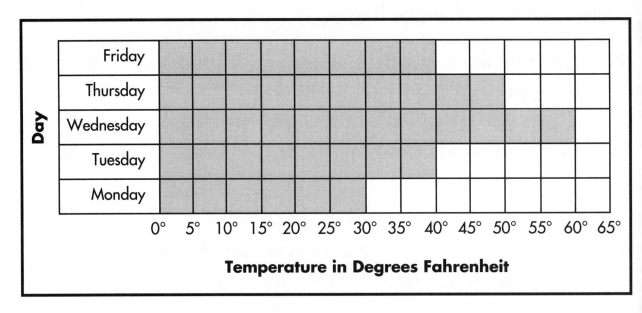

Temperature in Degrees Fahrenheit

1. Was the temperature higher on Monday or Thursday? _____ Thursday

2. Which two days had the same temperature? _____ Tuesday and Friday

3. Which day had the lowest temperature? _____ Monday

4. Which day had the highest temperature? _____ Wednesday

5. Tell how the temperature changed during the week.

The temperature got warmer until Wednesday. Then the temperature got cooler again.

Name _____

How Do We Measure Weather Conditions?

Complete each sentence.

1. A thermometer measures ___temperature___.

2. A ___rain gauge___ measures how much rain or snow has fallen.

3. An anemometer measures ___how fast___ the wind is blowing.

4. A wind vane measures ___which way___ the wind is blowing.

5. Circle what you will need on a cool and rainy day.

Match each picture to the word that tells about it.

6. cumulus cloud •

7. stratus cloud •

8. cirrus cloud •

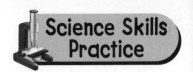

Classify

1. Classify these clothes by season by filling in the chart.

bathing suit	wool hat	shorts
sandals	mittens	snowsuit

Winter Clothing	Summer Clothing
snowsuit	shorts
mittens	sandals
wool hat	bathing suit

2. How did you classify the clothes? The clothes that help you stay warm are winter clothes. The clothes that help you stay cool are summer clothes.

Name _____

How Can We Prepare for Weather?

List two things you can do to prepare for each storm.

1.

hurricane

Bring loose items inside; go to a sheltered place.

2.

blizzard

Dress in layers of clothes; listen to radio warnings.

3.

tornado

Listen to radio warnings; seek shelter.

4.

thunderstorm

Stay away from trees; stay away from water.

Earth's Weather

Finish the word puzzle.

1. W
   A
2. T
3. T O R N A D O   8. S
   H   E   T
4. W E A T H E R 5. C R
   R   V   I   A
   M 6. E V A P O R A T E T
   O   P   R   U
   M   O   7. C U M U L U S
   E   R   S
   T
9. T E M P E R A T U R E
   R

Across
 3. A funnel-shaped cloud
 4. What the air outside is like
 6. What water does when it is warmed
 7. Puffy, white clouds seen in fair weather
 9. How hot or cold the air is

Down
 1. Water that is a gas (two words)
 2. A tool used to measure temperature
 5. Thin, feathery clouds seen when the weather is sunny
 8. Low, gray clouds that usually bring rain or snow

Name _____

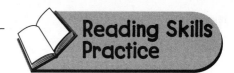

Sequence

Read each set of sentences.

> Winter is the coldest time of year. In some places it is cold enough to snow.
>
> In fall the air becomes cooler. The leaves of some trees change color and drop off.
>
> In spring the air is warmer. In some places it's rainy too. This helps new plants grow.
>
> Summer is the warmest time of year. It's often hot and sunny.

Rewrite the sets of sentences in the order of the seasons. The first set has been done for you.

1. In spring the air is warmer. In some places

it's rainy too. This helps new plants grow.

2. Summer is the warmest time of year. It's often

hot and sunny.

3. In fall the air becomes cooler. The leaves of some

trees change color and drop off.

4. Winter is the coldest time of year. In some places

it is cold enough to snow.

Name _____

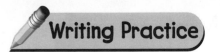

Tell a Tree's Story

Write to Express–Narrative Pretend that you are a tree. Tell the story of how you change through all four seasons. Draw pictures to go with your story. Use the story map to help plan your writing.

Character: _____ (kind of tree) _____ _____	Setting: _____ (where you live) _____ _____
Story	Pictures
What happens to the tree in spring? _____ _____	_____ _____
What happens to the tree in summer? _____ _____	_____ _____
What happens to the tree in fall? _____ _____	_____ _____
What happens to the tree in winter? _____ _____	_____ _____

Unit E, Chapter 1 Observing and Measuring Matter

LESSON 1
What Is Matter?

Three Forms of Matter

1. solid

2. liquid

3. gas

LESSON 2
What Can We Find Out About Solids?

Solid

1. has its own shape _____

2. has mass and length that can be _____
   measured

LESSON 3
What Can We Find Out About Liquids?

Liquid

1. flows to take the shape of its _____
   container

2. has mass that can be _____
   measured

LESSON 4
What Can We Find Out About Gases?

Gas

1. fills all the space inside its _____
   container

2. has mass that can be _____
   measured

Science Skills Practice

Classify

1. Classify these objects into two groups. List the objects in each group.

car

bicycle

carriage

shovel

football

basket

doll

skate

wheelbarrow

Objects With Wheels	Objects Without Wheels
car	shovel
carriage	doll
wheelbarrow	football
skate	basket
bicycle	

2. Circle the objects that have four wheels. car, carriage

3. Make an **X** on the objects that move people from place to place. car, carriage, skate, bicycle

What Is Matter?

Write **solid**, **liquid**, or **gas**.

1. solid _____

2. solid _____

3. liquid _____

4. gas _____

5. liquid _____

6. Color each object a different color.

  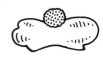

7. How are the objects alike? ___ all solids; all hats _____

8. How are they different? ___ different shapes, colors, _____
and sizes _____

Name _____

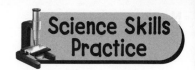

Order

1. How many dogs are there? _____ 1

2. How many fish are there? _____ 4

3. How many cats are there? _____ 3

4. Order the animals from least animals to most animals.

dogs   cats   fish
_____   _____   _____

5. Order these animals from smallest to largest.

bird

elephant

raccoon

bird   raccoon   elephant
_____   _____   _____
smallest   larger   largest

Name _____

What Can We Find Out About Solids?

Circle the word that tells about the property.

1. texture (soft) rough

2. shape  (sphere) cube

3. size large (small)

---

4. Color the containers that have solids in them. Children should color the cookie jar, the bucket, and bowl with ice cubes.

5. How long is this crayon? ____3____ inches

Name _____

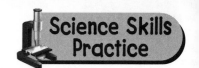

Measure

1. Sam is _____ 35 _____ inches tall.

2. Kim is _____ 50 _____ inches tall.

3. Tanya is _____ 40 _____ inches tall.

4. Mrs. Thomas is baking a cake. She needs 2 cups of milk.
Color how much milk she will need. Children should color
two of the three cups.

What Can We Find Out About Liquids?

Pretend you can pour the liquid from Container A into Container B. Draw how each liquid will look in Container B. Drawings should be same as Container B in each picture.

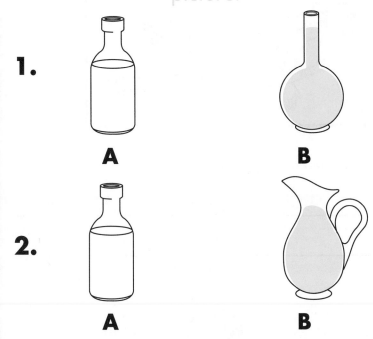

1.

A   B

2.

A   B

3. Fido was drinking his water. He knocked over his water dish. Draw what the spilled water will look like.
Water should be spread out over floor near dog's dish.

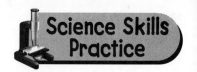

Infer

1. This man is scuba diving. Color where you think there
is air. Tank and breathing tube should be colored; bubbles
may also be colored.

2. How can the man breathe under water?

He breathes air from the tank.

_____

_____

3. Tell why the paper bag looks different in each picture.

The girl blew air into the bag to fill it up in the second

picture.

Name _____

What Can We Find Out About Gases?

Draw what these objects will look like when they are filled with air.

No Gas Inside	**Gas Inside**
1. balloon 	Children should draw a filled balloon.
2. beach ball 	Children should draw the beach ball rounded.
3. bubbles 	Children should draw filled bubbles.

4. Why are the firefighters wearing masks?

The masks keep the firefighters from breathing smoke
_____
or harmful gases.
_____

Observing and Measuring Matter

Complete each sentence with words from the box.

matter	mass	milliliter	centimeter	property

1. A door, a table, and even you are _____matter_____.

2. A _____centimeter_____ is a unit used to measure length.

3. A _____milliliter_____ is a unit used to measure a liquid.

4. The amount of matter in an object is its _____mass_____.

5. Color is a _____property_____ of matter.

Tell the type of matter in each container. Use words from the box.

liquid	solid	gas

6. _____solid_____ **7.** _____gas_____ **8.** _____liquid_____

Use with pages E4–E25.

Name _____

Cause and Effect

Liquids

A liquid does not have its own shape. It flows to take the shape of its container. A liquid in a bottle will have the same shape as the bottle. If a liquid is poured from one container to another, it will change to take the shape of the container it fills.

Look at the pictures and the statements. Circle the *cause*.

1.

The water will take the shape of the fish bowl.

2.

Rain formed this puddle.

Describe Properties of Matter

Write to Inform–Description Choose an object from the classroom. Draw the object in the box below. Then write sentences describing three properties of matter that you see in this object. Use the outline below to help you plan your sentences.

Drawing of Object

Outline of Sentences

Sentence 1	Property _____ Description _____
Sentence 2	Property _____ Description _____
Sentence 3	Property _____ Description _____

 Use with pages E28–E29.

Name _____

LESSON 1 What Happens When You Mix Matter?	LESSON 2 How Can Water Change?	LESSON 3 What Other Ways Does Matter Change?
1. Matter can be cut and mixed ____.	**Forms of Water** 1. solid 2. liquid 3. gas	**Kinds of Changes in Matter** 1. reversible change 2. irreversible change
2. Cutting and mixing does not change mass ____.	**What Changes Water's Form** 1. adding heat 2. taking away heat	

Name _____

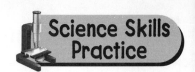

Observe

1. Tell how this person has changed.

The boy grew into an adult.

_____

_____

2. Observe the pictures. Record in the chart the things that changed and the things that did not change.

Things That Changed	Things That Did Not Change
All pieces of clothing should be listed.	The girl herself did not change.

Use with page E32.

Concept Review

What Happens When You Mix Matter?

 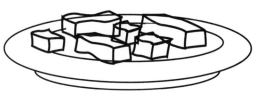

1. Maria's mom has two plates with the same amount of fudge. She cuts the fudge on one plate into small pieces. Which plate of fudge has more mass? Circle the letter of the best choice.

   a. the plate with small pieces of fudge

   b. the plate with the one large piece of fudge

   (c.) Neither: the cut fudge has the same mass as the single piece of fudge.

2. Tell what changed about the fudge. _the shape_____

3. You want to separate this mixture. Draw in the boxes the groups of nuts you would make.

   Children should draw one type of nut in each box.

     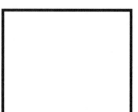 

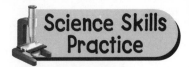

Plan an Investigation

1. This pie will be eaten by eight people. Think of a way to cut this pie into equal pieces for everyone. Draw your answer.

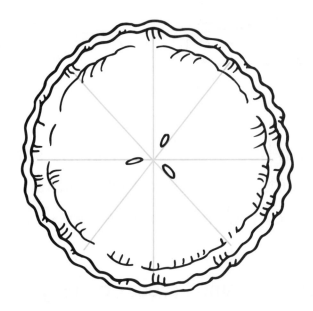

2. Steven gathered a bucket of snow. He wants to change the snow into a bucket of water. Draw Steven's bucket of snow where it will melt the fastest.

Children should draw the bucket near the fireplace.

Use with page E38.

Concept Review

How Can Water Change?

1. Color the temperatures at which water is a solid **blue**.

2. Color the temperatures at which water is a liquid **red**.

Children should color bottom to "0" blue, "0" to top red.

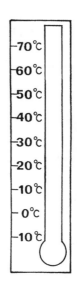

—70℃
—60℃
—50℃
—40℃
—30℃
—20℃
—10℃
— 0℃
—10℃

Tell whether water is a **liquid** or a **solid** in each picture. Then color the water in each picture.

3. __solid__   **4.** __liquid__   **5.** __liquid__

6. Tell what happens when heat is taken away from water.
It cools and changes to a solid (ice).
_____

7. Tell what happens when heat is added to liquid water.
It warms and changes to a gas (water vapor).
_____

8. What kind of change is it when matter can be changed back to the way it was? reversible
_____

Name _____

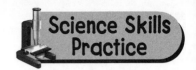

Predict

1. Draw what will happen next. Children should draw corn popping in the pan.

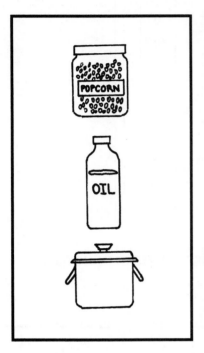  

2. Draw what will happen next. Drawings should indicate rain falling from dark clouds.

Name _____

What Other Ways Does Matter Change?

1. Joan made a log out of her clay. Then she rolled the clay into a ball. Now Joan doesn't want a ball. What can she do? Possible answer: Joan can change the shape of the clay back into a log.

_____

Decide if the change is **reversible** or **irreversible**.
Circle your answer.

2.    reversible   (irreversible)

3.    (reversible)   irreversible

4.    reversible   (irreversible)

5. (reversible)      **6.** reversible

    irreversible   (irreversible) 

7.    reversible   (irreversible)

Vocabulary Review

Changes in Matter

Circle **true** or **false**. If the sentence is false, change the underlined word or words to make it true.

1. Something made of two or more things is called a <u>reversible</u>.

true   (false)

mixture
_____

2. In a <u>reversible</u> change, something can be changed back to the way it was.

(true)   false

_____

3. Something that cannot be changed back to the way it was is called <u>mixture</u>.

true   (false)

irreversible
_____

Use the words from the box to label each picture.

| mixture | reversible | irreversible |

4. _reversible_

5. _irreversible_

6. _mixture_

Name _____

Identify Main Idea
and Supporting Details

Sam's Salad

Sam decided to make a salad using his favorite vegetables. There were several things he needed to do. First, he washed the lettuce. Next, he washed two carrots and two stalks of celery. He cut them into many small pieces. Then, he put all the things together in one big bowl. He used two big forks to mix it all up.

1. What is the main idea of the paragraph?

Sam is making a salad.

_____

_____

2. List the three things Sam does to make the salad.

Sam washes the vegetables.

Sam cuts the vegetables into small pieces.

Sam mixes all the vegetables together in one bowl.

3. How did all of Sam's favorite vegetables become a salad?

Sam made a mixture.

_____

_____

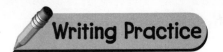

Write a Letter About A Taco

Write to Express–Friendly Letter Write a letter to a friend about a taco. In your letter, tell what things are mixed together to make a taco. Tell how these things are changed when a taco is prepared. Use the letter format below to help you plan your letter.

Heading

Today's date:

Greeting

Dear _____ ,

Body of Letter

First Paragraph (Parts of a taco):

Second Paragraph (How the parts are changed):

Closing

Your friend,

_____

Name _____

LESSON 1 What Are Forces? **Kinds of Forces** **1.** Wind and moving water push. **2.** gravity **3.** magnetism	LESSON 2 How Do Magnets Work? **1.** Opposite poles attract, and like poles repel. **2.** Magnets attract only some metals.	LESSON 3 How Can We Measure Motion? **1.** how far something moves **2.** how long something takes to move **3.** how much force it takes to move something

Unit F, Chapter 1 Forces and Motion

Name _____

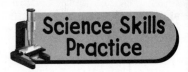

Observe

Write **push** or **pull** to tell how the person is
moving each object.

1. ____pull____   **2.** ____push____   **3.** ____pull____

4. ____push____   **5.** ____pull____

6. Draw yourself moving a ball.

> Drawings will vary but should show a child
> moving a ball by a push or pull.

7. Tell how you move a ball. ____Answers should include
moving a ball by a push or a pull.____
_____

Name _____

What Are Forces?

Match the objects to the words that tell how each moves.

1. magnetism •

2. moving air •

3. gravity •

4. moving air and
moving water •

5. How can you change the direction of an object that is
moving in a straight line?

You can change the direction of an object by pushing it
on one side.

_____

6. Circle the direction in which an object will go if you push it
on the right side.

(left)   straight   right

Use with page F11.   **Workbook • WB123**

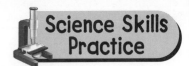

Form a Hypothesis

Use words from the box to write your hypothesis in a complete sentence.

magnet	attract	repel	paper clip

1. A magnet is brought near a paper clip.

Hypothesis: The magnet will attract the paper clip.

_____

_____

2. The *S* ends of two magnets are brought toward each other.

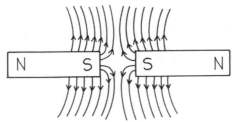

Hypothesis: The S ends of the magnets will repel each other.

_____

_____

Name _____

How Do Magnets Work?

1. Circle all of the objects that magnets attract.

(iron)　　　wood　　　cotton　　　(steel)

2. Why can magnets attract objects without touching them?

A magnet's pull can pass through air, water, and
_____
some solids.
_____

3. Label the remaining ends of the magnets below.

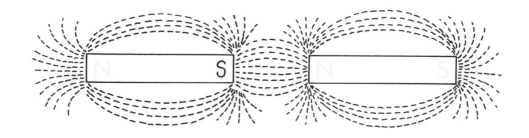

4. Circle all of the objects that are made with magnets.

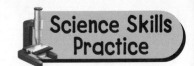

Use Numbers

Both these toy cars traveled across the floor.

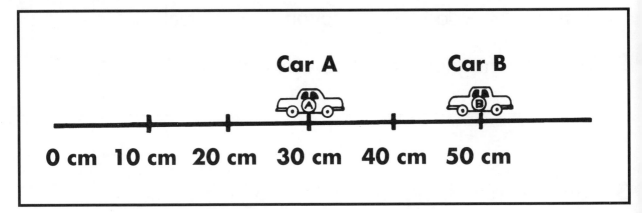

Car A   **Car B**

0 cm   10 cm   20 cm   30 cm   40 cm   50 cm

1. How far did Car A travel? ___30 centimeters___

2. How far did Car B travel? ___50 centimeters___

3. Which car traveled farther? ___Car B___

4. Which car was given a soft push? ___Car A___

5. Which car was given a hard push? ___Car B___

6. Tell how you know which car was pushed harder.

___The car that was pushed harder traveled farther.___

_____

_____

Name _____

How Can We Measure Motion?

1. The children kick the balls with the same force. Jenny's ball is heavier than Ana's ball. Circle what will happen.

    A Jenny's ball will go farther than Ana's ball.

    B Ana's ball will go farther than Jenny's ball.

    C Both balls will go the same distance.

Jenny   **Ana**

Match the motion to the words that tell how it is measured.

2. how far •

      •

3. how much time •

      •

4. how much force •

      •

Vocabulary
Review

Forces and Motion

Write the word that best completes each sentence.

1. A kite is moved by _____.

    water   gravity   wind

2. A _____ attracts iron objects.

    gravity   magnet   force

3. Susan will use a _____ to make something move.

    force   wind   water

4. When a dog moves, it is in _____.

    force   motion   wind

5. A ball rolls down a hill because of _____.

    gravity   magnet   wind

6. Write two sentences about this picture. Use the words **wind** and **water**.

Sentences will vary but should include a description of the "boat" being moved by forces including wind and water.

_____

_____

_____

Name _____

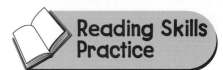

Cause and Effect

Forces in Daily Life

Mike and Cindy had a busy day. First, they took their dog Ben for a walk. Ben ran after a cat and tugged hard on the leash. The leash pulled Mike. Then, Mike and Cindy rode their bikes. Cindy pedaled very hard and went fast. When they got home, they had something to drink. Cindy knocked over her glass, and her drink spilled on the table.

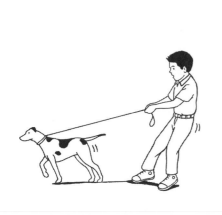

Use the story about Mike and Cindy to answer the questions.

1. What was the effect of Ben tugging on the leash?

The leash pulled Mike.

_____

2. What was the cause of Cindy riding her bike fast?

She pedaled very hard.

_____

3. What was the effect of the glass tipping over?

The drink spilled on the table.

_____

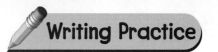

Tell How to Ride a Scooter

Write to Inform–How-To Write a paragraph that tells a younger child how to ride a scooter. Finish the sentences in the outline to help you think of three steps. Use motion words from the word bank for Steps 2 and 3.

push	pull	roll	turn

Step 1

Start with one foot . . .

on the scooter and one foot on the ground.

Step 2

Move forward by . . .

pushing off the ground with the foot that is not on the scooter until the wheels are rolling at a steady speed. Then pull this foot up so both feet are on the scooter.

Step 3

To change direction, . . .

turn the handlebar to the left or to the right.

Name _____

Unit F, Chapter 2 Hearing Sound

LESSON 1
What Is Sound?

1. Sound is made by _vibrations_.
2. Sound moves in every _direction_.
3. You hear sounds with your _ears_.

LESSON 2
How Do Sounds Vary?

Kinds of Sounds

1. loud or _soft_
2. high or _low_

LESSON 3
How Does Sound Travel?

What Sound Can Travel Through

1. gas
2. _liquid_
3. _solid_

LESSON 4
How Can We Make Different Sounds?

1. _Loud_ sounds use a lot of energy.
2. Soft sounds use _a little_ energy.

Plan an Investigation

Think of a way you could make a sound with each object.
Write your ideas.

plastic drink bottle

1. Squeeze it; blow in it.
_____
_____

wooden rolling pin

2. Roll it; tap with it.
_____
_____

can

3. Tap on it; drum it; roll it.
_____
_____

rubber band

4. Pluck it so it vibrates.
_____
_____

Name _____

What Is Sound?

1. Circle the things that make sound with vibrating strings.

Match the pictures to the words that tell how sound is made.

2.  •   • bell vibrates

3.  •   • wood vibrates

4.  •   • vocal cords vibrate

5. Jill is at a concert. How is she protecting her ears?

She is using ear plugs.

_____

_____

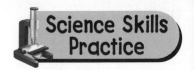
Science Skills
Practice

Observe

Match each object to the sound it makes.

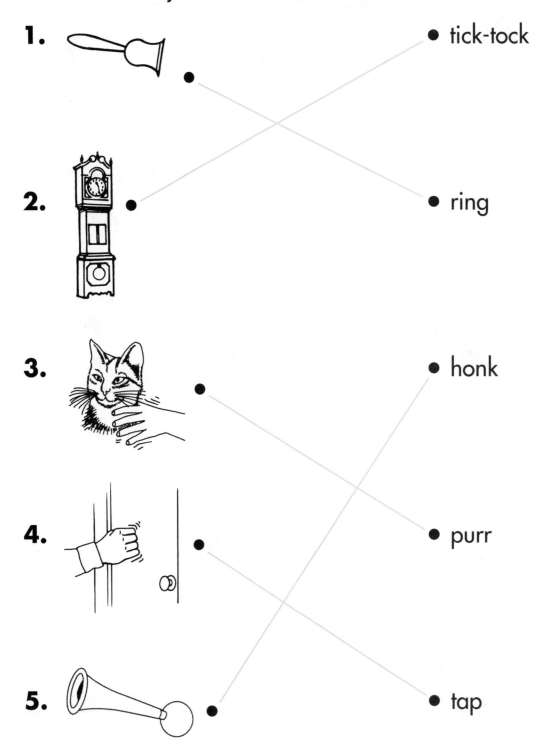

1. •   • tick-tock

2. •   • ring

3. •   • honk

4. •   • purr

5. •   • tap

     Use with page F36.

How Do Sounds Vary?

Describe each sound. Write **loud** or **soft**.

1. butterfly moving its wings _____ soft

2. fire truck siren _____ loud

3. jack hammer drilling _____ loud

4. boy whispering _____ soft

5. walking on carpet _____ soft

6. airplane taking off _____ loud

Circle **higher** or **lower** to finish each sentence.

7. A man's voice sounds _____
than a child's voice.   higher or (lower)

8. A lion's roar sounds _____
than a cat's meow.   higher or (lower)

9. A whistle sounds _____
than a truck engine.   (higher) or lower

10. A mouse's squeak sounds
_____ than a dog's bark.   (higher) or lower

Name _____

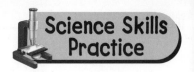

Predict

Jemal is calling Tumbles, his cat. The paw prints show each place Tumbles has been today.

1. Drawings should indicate Tumbles at the paw print closest to Jemal's door.

1. Find the paw print that shows the best place for Tumbles to hear Jemal calling. Draw Tumbles next to that paw print.

2. Tell why that is the best place for Tumbles to hear Jemal.

because the sound will travel a short distance to the
cat's ears
_____

3. Where might Tumbles not be able to hear Jemal at all? Mark an **X** on that spot. Children should mark the spot farthest away from Jemal.

4. Tell why Tumbles might not hear Jemal from that place.

because the sound has to travel a long way to reach
the cat's ears
_____

How Does Sound Travel?

Match the pictures to the words that tell how sound travels.

1. sound traveling • through air

2. sound traveling • through water

3. sound traveling through • a solid object

4. Draw an arrow from the boat's horn to all the places the sound of the horn will travel. *Arrows should flow from horn to surrounding air and water.*

5. Circle all the people who can hear the horn. *All the people should be circled.*

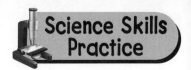

Compare

When you pour water into bottles and then tap the bottles, you hear sounds. The less water there is in the bottle, the higher the pitch of the sound is.

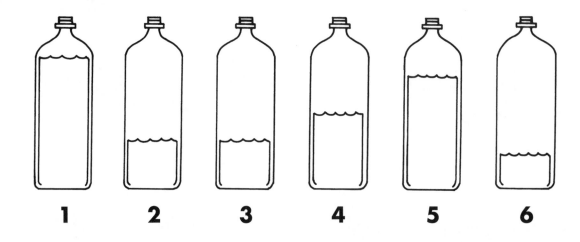

1   2   3   4   5   6

_____6_____ **1.** Which bottle would have the highest pitch?

____2 and 3____ **2.** Which two bottles would have the same pitch?

_____1_____ **3.** Which bottle would have the lowest pitch?

4. Circle the instruments that might sound similar.

Use with page F46.

How Can We Make Different Sounds?

1. Circle the thing that makes the lower sound.

Underline the word or words that make each sentence true.

2. Thin strings vibrate faster and make (higher   lower) sounds.

3. Making a string longer makes it vibrate (slower   faster) and sound (higher   lower).

4. If you use (a little   a lot of) energy to hit a drum hard, it makes a loud sound.

5. Tell about the energy the band members use to play loudly.
Answers should indicate the members of the band use
more energy when they play loudly.

Name _____

Hearing Sound

Match each word to its definition.

1. sound •

2. sonar •

3. pitch •

4. loudness •

• How loud or soft a sound is

• What is made when things vibrate

• Using sound to locate objects under water

• How high or low a sound is

Write the word from the box that completes each sentence.

music	vibrate

5. These instruments all make _____.

6. These parts of the instruments _____ and make sound.

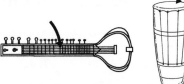

Name _____

Arrange Events in Sequence

How Sound Travels

Use the words in the box to answer the questions.

drum	ears	air

1. What is vibrating? _____ drum

2. What is the sound traveling through? _____ air

3. What does the sound travel to? _____ ears

Write three sentences that tell how the sound travels when the boy plays the drum.

Accept reasonable answers.

_____

_____

_____

Use with page F43.   **Workbook • WB141**

Write a Speech About Music

Write to Persuade–Opinion Write a short speech about your favorite kind of music. Give two reasons why people should like this kind of music. In your speech, tell what kind of instruments are used to make this kind of music. Tell whether this music is usually loud or soft. Use the outline below to help you plan your speech.

Your favorite kind of music: _____
_____

Instruments used: _____
_____

Is the music usually loud or soft? _____
_____

One reason why people should like this kind of music: _____
_____

Another reason why people should like this kind of music: ___
_____

Repeat your opinion with different words: _____
_____

Unit Experiments
Grade 2

Introduction to Unit Experiments 144

UNIT A

Plants and Light 147

UNIT B

Plants and Pollution 150

UNIT C

Plants and Erosion 153

UNIT D

Puddle Shape and Evaporation 156

UNIT E

Water and Rusting 159

UNIT F

Metals and Magnets 162

1. Observe and ask a question.

_____

_____

_____

2. Form a hypothesis.

A hypothesis is a suggested answer to the question you are investigating. You must be able to do a fair test of the hypothesis.

_____

_____

3. Plan a fair test.

What things will you keep the same in the test? Write or draw them here.

4. What is one thing you will change in the test?

_____

_____

_____

_____

5. What things will you need to do the test? List or draw them here.

6. What steps will you take to do the test?

_____

_____

_____

_____

_____

7. Do the test.

Record your data in a chart.

8. Draw conclusions. Communicate results.

What are your results? How can you communicate your results to others?

_____

_____

_____

_____

_____

_____

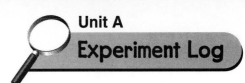
Plants and Light

Observe and ask a question.

1. What can you ask about the way light changes the growth of plants?

How does light change the way plants grow?

_____

_____

Form a hypothesis.

2. What is something you think is true about the way light changes the growth of plants?

Light helps a plant grow.

_____

_____

Plan a fair test.

3. What things will you keep the same in the test?

I will use identical plants. Both plants will be put in the same place. I will give both plants the same amount and temperature of water.

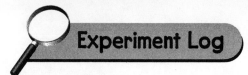
4. What one thing will you change in the test?

I will change the amount of light that each plant gets. One

plant will get light. The other will not get light.

5. What things will you need to do the test?
List or draw them here.

2 shoe boxes, marker, 2 identical plants in pots,

centimeter ruler, black paper, tap water, measuring cup

6. What steps will you take to do the test?

a. Place the plants in shoe boxes labeled A and B.

b. Measure and record the height of each plant. Observe

and record the number and color of each plant's leaves.

c. Cover one plant with black paper so that it gets no light.

d. Keep both plants in the same place. Give the plants the same

amount of water every other day.

e. After one week, remove the black paper. Repeat Step b.

f. Do the test again for one more week.

Name _____

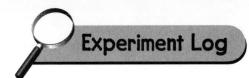

Do the test.

7. Record your data in the chart.

How does light change the way plants grow?

Week	Plant A	Plant B
Week 1	Height— Number of Leaves— Color of Leaves—	Height— Number of Leaves— Color of Leaves—
Week 2	Height— Number of Leaves— Color of Leaves—	Height— Number of Leaves— Color of Leaves—

Draw conclusions. Communicate results.

8. What are your results? How can you communicate your results to others?

_____

_____

_____

_____

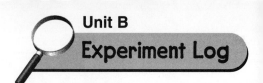

Plants and Pollution

Observe and ask a question.

1. What can you ask about the way polluted water changes plants?

How does polluted water change plants?

Are some kinds of polluted water more harmful than others?

_____

Form a hypothesis.

2. What is something you think is true about the way polluted water changes plants?

Polluted water harms plants.

_____

Plan a fair test.

3. What things will you keep the same in the test?

I will use the same kind of plants. I will use tap water.

I will put the plants in places with the same amount

of sunlight.

Name _____

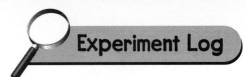

4. What one thing will you change in the test?

I will change the type of water used.

5. What things will you need to do the test?
List or draw them here.

3 plants, 3 containers, water, detergent, oil, measuring

cup, tablespoon, marker

6. What steps will you take to do the test?

a. Label the containers A, B, and C. Place one plant in each

container. Observe the plants. Record observations.

b. Pour 3 cups of water into Plant A.

c. Pour 3 cups of water and 1 tablespoon of detergent into

Plant B.

d. Pour 3 cups of water and 1 tablespoon of mineral oil into

Plant C.

e. Observe the plants again. Record observations.

f. After 3 days, and then again after 1 week, observe the

plants and record observations.

Name _____

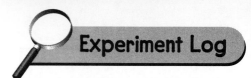

Do the test.

7. Record your data in the chart.

How Did the Plants Look?

Plant	Day 1	After 3 Days	After 1 Week
Plant A			
Plant B			
Plant C			

Draw conclusions. Communicate results.

8. What are your results? How can you communicate your results to others?

_____

_____

_____

_____

_____

Name _____

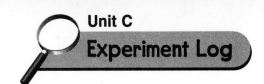

Plants and Erosion

Observe and ask a question.

1. What can you ask about the way plants might change how soil is washed away?

Do plants change the amount of soil that is washed

away by water?

Form a hypothesis.

2. What is something you think is true about plants and soil erosion?

Plants help keep soil from being eroded by water.

Plan a fair test.

3. What things will you keep the same in the test?

I will keep the amount of soil, the size and shape of the pans, and the amount and temperature of water the same. I will add the water from the same height each time. I will keep the slope of the pans the same. I will sprinkle the water onto the soil the same way each time. I will keep the measuring cup and the kind of watering can the same.

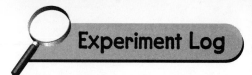
4. What one thing will you change in the test?

One pan of soil will have plants (grass) growing in it.

5. What things will you need to do your test? List or draw them here.

2 pans, soil, measuring cup, watering can, room-temperature

water, centimeter ruler, piece of sod or grass seeds

6. What steps will you take to do the test?

a. Place the soil into one end of one pan. Prop up the end of the

pan that has the soil.

b. Fill the watering can with 2 cups of water.

c. Hold the watering can about 20 cm above the pan. Make it

"rain" on the soil.

d. Observe how much soil is washed away to the other end of

the pan.

e. Put the piece of sod in one end of the other pan. Prop up the

end of the pan that has the sod.

f. Repeat Steps b–d.

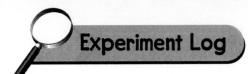

Do the test.

7. Draw pictures to show what happened to each sample of soil.

Draw conclusions. Communicate results.

8. What are your results? How can you communicate your results to others?

_____

_____

_____

_____

_____

_____

_____

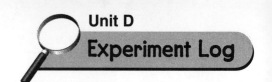
Puddle Shape and Evaporation

Observe and ask a question.

1. What can you ask about the way the shape of a puddle changes?

Will water in a deep puddle evaporate faster than the same

amount of water in a shallow puddle?

Form a hypothesis.

2. What is something you think is true about the way the shape of a puddle changes evaporation?

Water in a shallow puddle will evaporate faster than the same

amount of water in a deep puddle.

Plan a fair test.

3. What things will you keep the same in the test?

I will put the same amount and temperature of water in each

puddle. I will put the puddles in the same place. I will measure

at the same time every day with the same measuring cup.

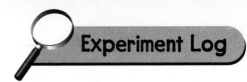

4. What one thing will you change in the test?

The model puddles will have different shapes.

5. What things will you need to do your test?
Write or draw them here.

measuring cup, room-temperature water, clear plastic cup;

clear, shallow plastic bowl; clear plastic saucer;

sunny windowsill

6. What steps will you take to do the test?

a. Pour equal amounts of room-temperature water into the

cup, the bowl, and the saucer.

b. Put the cup, the bowl, and the saucer on a sunny windowsill.

c. Every day for 5 days, pour the water from each container,

one at a time, into the measuring cup. Measure and record the

amount of water. Then pour the water back into the same

container it came from.

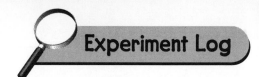
Do the test.

7. Record your data in the chart.

How Does Puddle Shape Affect Evaporation?

Day	Amount of Water		
	Cup	**Bowl**	**Saucer**
Monday			
Tuesday			
Wednesday			
Thursday			
Friday			

Draw conclusions. Communicate results.

8. What are your results? How can you communicate your results to others?

_____

_____

_____

_____

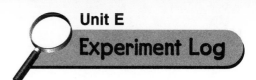
Water and Rusting

Observe and ask a question.

1. What can you ask about the way water helps make things rust?

Does water make some things rust faster?

Does water make steel wool rust faster?

Form a hypothesis.

2. What is something you think is true about the way water helps make objects rust?

Water will help make steel wool rust faster.

Plan a fair test.

3. What things will you keep the same in the test?

I will use 2 identical pieces of steel wool. I will wrap both

pieces of steel wool in the same kind and number of

paper towels.

I will observe the pieces of steel wool for the same amount

of time.

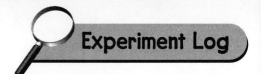
4. What one thing will you change in the test?

One paper towel will be wet, and the other one will be dry.

5. What objects will you need to do the test? Write or draw them here.

2 pieces of steel wool, paper towels, water, 2 paper plates

6. What steps will you take to do the test?

a. Wrap one piece of steel wool in a dry paper towel and place on a paper plate.

b. Wrap the other piece of steel wool in a wet paper towel and place on a paper plate.

c. Add a little water to the wet paper towel every other day.

d. After one week, unwrap and observe the steel wool. Rewrap.

e. After two weeks, check again to see whether rust has formed on either piece of steel wool.

Name _____

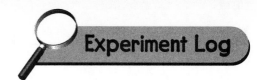

Do the test.

7. Record your data in the chart.

Does water help make steel wool rust?

Steel Wool	After 1 Week	After 2 Weeks
steel wool with water		
steel wool with no water		

Draw conclusions. Communicate results.

8. What are your results? How can you communicate your results to others?

_____

_____

_____

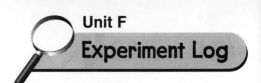
Metals and Magnets

Observe and ask a question.

1. What can you ask about the way magnets work?

What metals do magnets attract? Are all metals attracted
to magnets?

_____

Form a hypothesis.

2. What is something you think is true about how magnets attract metal?

Magnets attract every kind of metal.

_____

Plan a fair test.

3. What things will you keep the same in the test?

I will use the same magnet to test all the objects. All the
objects I test will be made of metal. All the objects will be
about the same size and mass.

_____

_____

4. What one thing will you change in the test?

I will change the kinds of metal tested.

The objects I test will be made of different kinds of metal.

5. What things will you need to do the test?
Write or draw them here.

magnet, different metal objects

6. What steps will you take to do the test?

a. I will hold the magnet near each metal object.

b. I will observe whether each object is attracted to the

magnet.

Name _____

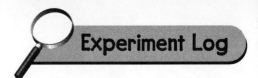

Do the test.

7. Record your data in the chart.

What metal objects does a magnet attract?

Metal Object	Attracted to Magnet?

Draw conclusions. Communicate results.

8. What are your results? How can you communicate your results to others?

_____

_____

_____

_____